Quotable
SPURRIER

Quotable
SPURRIER

**The Nerve, Verve, and Victorious Words of
and about STEVE SPURRIER,
America's Most Scrutinized Football Coach**

Gene Frenette

TowleHouse Publishing
Nashville, Tennessee

TowleHouse books are distributed by National Book Network (NBN), 4720 Boston Way, Lanham, Maryland 20706.

Library of Congress Cataloging-in-Publication Data

Spurrier, Steve, 1945–
   Quotable Spurrier : the nerve, verve, and victorious words of and about Steve Spurrier, America's most scrutinized football coach / [compiled by] Gene Frenette.
      p. cm.6 -- (Potent quotables)
Includes bibliographical references (p.).
   ISBN 1-931249-17-2 (alk. paper)
   1. Spurrier, Steve, 1945---Quotations. 2. Football coaches--United States--Quotations. 3. Football--Coaching--Quotations, maxims, etc. I. Frenette, Gene. II. Title. III. Series.
   GV939.S65 A32 2002
   796.332'092--dc21

                                                                2002008803

Cover design by Gore Studio, Inc.
Page design by Mike Towle

Printed in the United States of America
1 2 3 4 5 6 — 06 05 04 03 02

No book is possible without the patience and sacrifice of many people, especially an understanding family. I wish to commend my wife, Dot, and children, Sean, Joey, Kelly, and Matthew, for being team players for the time invested in the project.

CONTENTS

ACKNOWLEDGMENTS

THANKS GO TO THE following people and groups for their assistance or consent in putting together this book: Norm Carlson, University of Florida assistant athletic director for communications; the *Florida Times-Union*; and the University of Florida sports information office.

INTRODUCTION

I F ANYTHING HAS DRIVEN Steve Spurrier to become one of the most compelling coaching figures of his generation, it's being told that he can't do something.

Anyone who has followed his career—particularly his stops at Duke, the Tampa Bay Bandits of the United States Football League, and at his alma mater, the University of Florida—knows that the controversial and ultrasuccessful ball coach lives to prove people wrong.

Spurrier is an icon in his profession, as well as a favorite target of critics, because he never wavers in his confidence that his coaching style can win anywhere and produce championship teams on the college or professional level.

In fact, one of the main reasons the brash, self-assured Spurrier left a secure job at Florida—where his teams went 122-27-1 in twelve years and won six Southeastern Conference titles—for the Washington Redskins is he wanted the challenge of showing people that he can succeed in football's biggest proving ground: the NFL.

Because just as skeptics doubted him at all his previous head-coaching stops, many were certain going into the 2002 NFL season that Spurrier would be humbled as he made the ultimate career jump. They believed that his passing schemes that worked so well at Florida and Duke had a lesser chance of succeeding in the NFL, where thirty-one other teams have fairly equal resources and opposing coaches are less apt to be fooled by the man known derisively in some circles as "the Evil Genius."

That's precisely the kind of thinking Spurrier loves to hear and read about. Know this: He files mental notes about anyone who says or writes something that he construes to be questioning his ability.

When Spurrier wrote me a letter after he got the Redskins job, expressing his appreciation for a magazine article I wrote about his tenure at Florida, he added this reminder: "We've had a good relationship over the years, even though you thought the Gators should hire Howard Schnellenberger. You know I remember everything."

It doesn't matter if it's football, golf, Ping-Pong, or doubting journalists, Spurrier always carries that I'll-show'em attitude. And when it comes to coaching, nobody enjoys the opportunity of testing his skills as an offensive chess master quite like Spurrier.

One of his favorite quotes is from George Bernard Shaw, and it speaks volumes about his coaching career: "You see things and you say, 'Why?' But I dream things that never were and I say, 'Why not?'"

In 1966, many believe Spurrier put a lock on the Heisman Trophy when he kicked a thirty-yard field goal in the closing seconds to beat Auburn. How many quarterbacks who had never been in that position would have the confidence to convince the coaching staff to let him even attempt that kick? Despite the laces facing him when the ball was put on the tee, Spurrier delivered.

Much of his twenty-four-year coaching career has followed the same script—proving you can win without having to do everything by the book.

When Spurrier became the youngest pro head coach in the USFL at age thirty-seven, he led the Bandits to two play-off berths with the most innovative passing attack that three-year-old league ever saw. Spurrier's reputation as a master tutor of quarterbacks was enhanced when he pulled former NFL washout John Reaves out of a real estate job and turned him into one of the USFL's most productive quarterbacks.

At Duke, the doubters followed Spurrier again, insisting it was a basketball school that was always destined to be mediocre on the gridiron. Well, in Spurrier's third and last season in Durham, North Carolina, the Blue Devils won their first ACC Championship since 1962 because defenses never could put the brakes on his intricate passing offense. Duke set an all-time ACC record of 501.7 yards total offense per game.

When Florida offered him its coaching job, all Spurrier heard was how Southeastern Conference championships were won with defense and a running game, not throwing the ball all over the field. He heard about Florida's history of under-achieving and how archrival Georgia had their number. Spurrier was playing in a different league now, and his offensive philosophy, critics insisted, wouldn't work as well. Upon his arrival, he discovered a team so accustomed to running the ball with Emmitt Smith, the quarterbacks didn't know how to call an audible. Wide receiver Tre Everett said the duties of his position were considered so minor that the receivers thought of themselves as little offensive linemen.

By the time Spurrier was through at Florida twelve years later, everything had changed. His teams had rewritten virtually every school and SEC passing record. They had won a national championship in 1996. And they had gone 11-1 against Georgia.

Spurrier's belief in his unique system clearly wasn't for everybody. He interviewed for head-coaching jobs at LSU, Mississippi State, and California, and was rejected each time before landing the Duke job.

Ultimately, his twelve-year reign at Florida proved that his willingness to attack defenses with a wide-open brand of football could stand the test of time, and it also reshaped the philosophy of college football's preeminent conference. Many now believe that his influence on the college game was so far-reaching that Spurrier ranks only behind Alabama legend Paul Bear Bryant in terms of a lasting legacy in the SEC.

Before he ever took the Florida job, Spurrier's wife, Jerri, had this telling remark about her husband's future: "I don't see failure coming to Steve's coaching career. He's too consistent and uncomplicated."

As Spurrier embarks on what is likely his last coaching challenge with the Washington Redskins, the fifty-seven-year-old coach still retains a bit of those boyish looks. He also flashes that trademark grin, or maybe it's a smirk, at critics who think this venture into the NFL won't be nearly as successful a journey as his past eighteen seasons as a head coach. Stephen Orr Spurrier has the appropriate initials (SOS) for a man who has come to the rescue of every football program that he's ever commanded.

Now it's on to the next rescue mission in Washington, D.C., with the Redskins, the team that he watched most on television as a kid growing up in Johnson City, Tennessee.

Go ahead, tell him he can't get it done in the NFL. History says you'll just be playing right into his hands.

—*Gene Frenette*

Playing Days

COLLEGIATE PLAYING DAYS

I probably would have rather beaten Georgia and won the first SEC Championship for all of us (than win the Heisman Trophy). If there's one game I'll remember, it's probably the one we lost.[1]

—referring to 27-10 defeat to Georgia in 1966

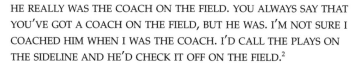

HE REALLY WAS THE COACH ON THE FIELD. YOU ALWAYS SAY THAT YOU'VE GOT A COACH ON THE FIELD, BUT HE WAS. I'M NOT SURE I COACHED HIM WHEN I WAS THE COACH. I'D CALL THE PLAYS ON THE SIDELINE AND HE'D CHECK IT OFF ON THE FIELD.[2]

—Ray Graves, *former Florida coach*

BLINDFOLDED, WITH HIS BACK TO THE WALL, WITH HIS HANDS
TIED BEHIND HIM, STEVE SPURRIER WOULD BE A TWO-POINT
FAVORITE AT HIS OWN EXECUTION.

*—**John Logue**, the* Atlanta Journal, *after Spurrier
rallied Florida to a 17-10 victory over North Carolina State in 1966*

I caught it decent. Just a low end-over-ender. It wasn't
real high. It just cleared (the crossbar) by maybe three
yards or so.[3]

*—about his game-winning, thirty-yard
field goal that beat Auburn, 30-27, in 1966*

HEISMAN TROPHY

I think I appreciate it more as the years go by. And you
also appreciate the other fellows who have won it more.
I've really come to enjoy being with them at the banquet.[4]

WHEN YOU LOOK BACK THROUGH THE YEARS, I'M SURE THE
BIGGEST PRIZE HE GOT THAT YEAR (IN 1966) WAS JERRI RATHER
THAN THE HEISMAN. SHE'S DONE A WHOLE LOT MORE FOR HIM
THAN THAT HEISMAN.[5]

—**Fred Goldsmith**, *former Duke football coach and the
witness at Spurrier's wedding ceremony after Steve and Jerri's elopement*

There's not much chance to celebrate. We've got Miami to
think about, and you can't let up before a game like that.

—*after learning he won the Heisman Trophy
just before a midweek practice prior to the Miami game*

I believe more people can see it at the university than if I
keep it myself.[6]

—*explaining why he gave the Heisman Trophy to University of
Florida president J. Wayne Reitz shortly after receiving the award*

WINLESS 1976 TAMPA BAY BUCCANEERS

That year was good for me, it really was. It was a tremendous learning experience. In life, you either bounce back stronger from adversity or you go the other way. I like to think that's the year that helped me later on get into coaching.[7]

We had a bunch of ragtag players out there, boy. When your expectations are not real high—and that's a sad way to be—losing becomes a habit for a lot of players and coaches.[8]

NFL PLAYING CAREER

I can write off 1967. It has not been especially enjoyable or educational. I blame myself for two things: I wasn't prepared, and I haven't improved a bit since college.[9]

—after struggling through his rookie season with the San Francisco 49ers

I probably didn't put forth the maximum effort when I was at San Francisco (with the 49ers). I wasn't a real pusher. I probably should have been a little more ambitious.[10]

—about spending most of his nine seasons with the 49ers as a benchwarmer

I think I certainly needed to be under somebody who really pushed you because I was not a self-motivator at that time. Some other times in my life, I was. But as a pro player, I was not very good at pushing myself in the off-season. I played a lot of golf and didn't work out too much.[11]

After that, I was terrible. I couldn't get myself up for the games the way I got myself up for that game. I just didn't do it.[12]

—about never again performing like the quarterback
who threw three TD passes to lead the 49ers to
a 24-23 victory over the Los Angeles Rams in 1975

I was real limited. I didn't have a real strong arm, and I wasn't real mobile.[13]

—*on why he rode the bench for most of his ten NFL seasons*

~

When they went with (Norm) Snead last year, I was pretty bitter. That's the only bad memory I have of San Francisco.[14]

—*on not inheriting the San Francisco 49ers'*
starting job after John Brodie's retirement

~

PEOPLE AROUND US STARTED BOOING AND LISA STARTED BOOING, TOO. I SAID, "LISA, WHY ARE YOU BOOING?" SHE SAID, "I DON'T KNOW, BECAUSE EVERYBODY ELSE IS." I SAID, "DO YOU KNOW WHO THEY'RE BOOING? THEY'RE BOOING YOUR FATHER."[15]

—***Jerri Spurrier*** *on her nine-year-old daughter's booing during*
a 1976 Tampa Bay Buccaneers game in which Steve was the quarterback

~

Steve Spurrier as seen during his heyday as the University of Florida quarterback, on his way to winning the Heisman Trophy. (Photo courtesy of University of Florida sports information office)

WITH THE ACQUISITION OF GARY HUFF, WE THINK STEVE SPURRIER
SHOULD BE GIVEN THIS OPPORTUNITY TO GO TO THE TEAM OF HIS
CHOICE, INSTEAD OF TRADING HIM TO A TEAM HE MIGHT NOT
WANT TO GO TO. WE WISH HIM THE BEST.[16]

—**John McKay**, *former Tampa Bay Buccaneers
coach, about putting Spurrier on waivers*

I haven't lost any confidence or I'd hang it up. I think my
passing has gotten better the past few years. I feel more
like I'm twenty.[17]

—*after signing with the Denver Broncos on June 2, 1977*

Yeah, there's a lot of lousy quarterbacks around. Somebody
can use me.[18]

—*after being released by the Denver Broncos on August 30, 1977*

I got cut by three teams in 1977. That's when I went back to
Gainesville to watch the Gators play. I had to do something.[19]

HE HAD OFFERS TO BE A
CAR SALESMAN. THAT
WAS THE BEST OFFER HE
HAD, TO SELL CARS IN
JACKSONVILLE OR OCALA.[20]

—**Jerri Spurrier**, *after Steve was released by the Miami Dolphins in 1977*

Career Moves

CAREER CHOICES

I always figured I'd play as long as I could (in the NFL) and then get a job in public relations or something. I wasn't good enough to make money as a golfer. But I surely hadn't prepared myself to be a coach.[1]

〜

No matter where I wind up, we'll have fun. I'm pretty uncomplicated. I just do what comes natural. I'm one coach who'll never suffer burnout. Not the way I approach the game.[2]

〜

I thought maybe I had a chance as a coach. I had been around some good coaches and some sorry coaches. If some of those sorry coaches could make a living, I had a chance.[3]

—*on why he chose coaching as a profession*

I can say I'm going to spend four or five hours at
night looking at films, but people won't believe
me until I actually do it. I think coaching is
something I'm going to like doing.[4]

*—after accepting his first coaching job as
an offensive assistant at Florida under Doug Dickey*

I realize that they've got to do what they've
got to do—look around the nation and find the
best coach they can. The timing of it is not good
for me.[5]

—after withdrawing his name from consideration for the Florida job in 1984

You can make substantially more money in the
pros, but this is where I wanted to be.

*—at his introductory press conference as
Florida's new coach on December 31, 1990*

EVERY BIG DECISION HE'S MADE, EVEN SOME I COULDN'T BELIEVE, HAS ALWAYS TURNED OUT RIGHT. WHEN HE TOOK THE (TAMPA BAY) BANDITS JOB, I THOUGHT, "AHHHH, THIS IS LIKE THE WORLD FOOTBALL LEAGUE." BUT IT TURNED OUT TO BE THE MOST FUN TIME WE EVER HAD. I DIDN'T HAVE ANYTHING TO DO WITH THAT DECISION, WHICH IS FINE. I JUST PACKED THE BOXES.[6]

—Jerri Spurrier

When I left Duke, my athletic director, Tom Butters, told me, "Steve, you're a big ol' hero down there, and all you can do is go down there and mess it up." Well, I don't see it that way. I've got so much confidence in my coaching ability that failure is not even a consideration.[7]

I'm thankful that I did need a job. I had made a little money in the NFL. It's amazing when you think about it. I'm the only ten-year NFL guy who is coaching at all. How I got here is a strange and very, very fortunate set of events.[8]

—about getting his first coaching job,
as a Florida assistant under Doug Dickey, in 1978

Spurrier's reputation as a master in the area of quarterback develop-
ment was already well deserved by the time he got to Duke. (Photo
courtesy of University of Florida sports information office)

I've been fairly bored and golfed-out four months ago. I was pretty much sitting around doing nothing.[9]

—from his introductory news conference in 1987 as Duke's head coach

After we beat North Carolina, 41-0, in the last game of the '89 season, I told our players that I was going to be their coach through the bowl game, but that I couldn't guarantee that I'd be with them after that. The opportunity and challenge to coach at the University of Florida was something I could not turn down. I believe the players and fans of Duke have come to understand that my decision to accept the Florida job was one that I had to make.[10]

I'm not burned out, stressed out, or mentally fatigued from coaching. I just feel my career as a college head coach after fifteen years is complete, and if the opportunity and challenge of coaching an NFL team happens, it is something I would like to pursue.

—farewell press conference at Florida, January 7, 2002

I just told him I've got the best job I can think of in coaching. I have no intention of ever leaving Florida.[11]

—in 1993, about declining to interview with general manager John Beake about the Denver Broncos' coaching vacancy

I don't want a ten-year or lifetime contract. I might get lazy or complacent. We all have to be accountable from week to week, season to season, and year to year. A college or university, if they don't like their coach, they should be in position to get rid of him. They shouldn't be stuck with a coach they don't want. And if a coach isn't happy where he is, he ought to be able to leave, too.[12]

—during a 1993 pre-Sugar Bowl news conference

I want to be able to walk out of here. I don't want to have to run out. Have you looked at the coaching history of the University of Florida? This job has chewed up and spit out about every coach it's had over the last seventy-five years. I don't want to be chewed up and spit out.[13]

—after announcing his resignation at Florida

They have to compete with pro football up there. Maryland has trouble getting on the sports page, so they not only want a new coach who can win, but they want one who can put on a pretty good show to get people back in the stadium.[14]

—after applying for the vacant Maryland job in 1981

~

It's a great school that plays in the best conference in the country, no matter what those folks from the SEC say.[15]

—in 1986 after interviewing for the head-coaching job at California

~

The Tampa Bay Bandits have been good to Steve Spurrier. It's not the best thing for me. I don't think it would be right leaving a month before our season starts.[16]

—after he withdrew his name from consideration for the Florida job following Charley Pell's resignation in 1984

~

AFTER THE USFL FOLDED, THE PLACES STEVE WENT TO INTERVIEW FOR JOBS (CALIFORNIA, LSU, AND MISSISSIPPI STATE) NEVER SEEMED TO BE RIGHT. BUT HE WASN'T DISAPPOINTED BECAUSE HE ALWAYS FELT LIKE SOMETHING RIGHT MIGHT HAPPEN. HE'S SUCH AN OPTIMIST.[17]

—*Jerri Spurrier*

I had a fascination of some day coaching the Bucs, the only NFL team I had any interest in coaching. It came and it was time to listen, but not to leave. Make it clear, I am not rejecting, not turning down the Bucs, I am staying at Florida. Big difference. I find our roots are just too deep.[18]

—*after changing his mind in 1996 and turning down the chance to coach the Tampa Bay Buccaneers*

Maybe this will end the speculation for years to come. I've talked and I've listened, and I think I'm just a college ball coach. That's what's best for me. I did my little fling. I'm a Gator and I hope to be for many years. I doubt if I'll have another NFL opportunity, but I'm not looking for one.[19]

—*after turning down the Bucs job*

I've said it before and I'll say it again: A coach should never say "never" or "always."[20]

GETTING FIRED

I WAS WELL AWARE OF STEVE'S BEING A HERO IN THE MINDS OF THE FLORIDA PEOPLE, BUT I WAS ALSO AWARE HE HAD WORKED HARD TO GET THE HEAD-COACHING JOB. THERE'S AN OLD RULE IN COACHING THAT IT'S NOT GOOD TO RETAIN THE COACH WHO BATTLES FOR THE HEAD JOB. THAT WAS THE ONLY REASON I HAD ANY DOUBTS ABOUT RETAINING STEVE. I FELT IT WOULD BE A CLEANER, MORE CLEAR-CUT TRANSITION BY NOT HAVING HIM ON THE STAFF.[21]
—*Charley Pell*, *former Florida coach, on why he didn't retain Spurrier on Florida's staff after taking over for Doug Dickey*

I knew I'd be gone. He's a sprint-out coach and that's not my style. It didn't shock me at all.[22]
—*reacting to not being retained by Charley Pell*

From 1977, I was released by
three NFL teams. I wasn't
kept by Charley Pell (at
Florida) or Bill Curry (at
Georgia Tech). . . . I'll show
those people they were wrong,
the ones who didn't keep me
as a coach. We all like to
prove people wrong who say
we're no good.[23]

I WAS IN THE PROCESS OF MAKING UP MY MIND BETWEEN TWO OR
THREE PEOPLE, AND HE WAS ONE OF THEM, BUT HE TOOK THE
DUKE COORDINATOR'S JOB. I DIDN'T KNOW HIM AS A FOOTBALL
COACH AT THAT TIME. I DIDN'T KNOW HE WAS A GENIUS. HAD I
KNOWN THEN WHAT I KNOW NOW, I WOULD HAVE HIRED HIM.[24]
— **Bill Curry**, *former Georgia Tech coach, on why he didn't
immediately retain Spurrier after taking the Tech job from Pepper Rodgers*

WE'VE BEEN OUT OF A JOB FIVE TIMES OVER THE YEARS, AND
NONE OF IT WAS DEVASTATING. I DON'T KNOW WHY, BUT I WAS
NEVER AFRAID. WE NEVER PANICKED. I DON'T EVER REMEMBER
PANICKING.[25]

— **Jerri Spurrier**

USFL DAYS

The reason I got to be the head coach of the Bandits was
because our offense had done well at Duke. I don't think it
would be too smart of me to go out and hire an offensive
coordinator and turn it over to him. That's my deal.[26]

We got the kickoff (in his first game coaching the Tampa Bay Bandits) and came out in the no-huddle offense. I don't think many fans, if any, had ever seen the no-huddle offense. Most people think it started with the Cincinnati Bengals, but I believe the Bandits were one of the first teams to use it. The USFL fans really appreciated the way we would gamble, not always playing everything by the book.[27]

My wife was a little skeptical. It was a new league and sometimes those things don't last more than a year or so. But with the TV contract the USFL had with ABC, there was a lot of stability and credibility. And it was an opportunity to be a head coach. If I did well, there would be other teams looking for a head coach.[28]

We played stupid football all year.[29]

—after his 1983 Tampa Bay Bandits lost to Birmingham and finished the season 11-7 and out of the play-offs

That's the biggest slump of any team I've ever been on.[30]
> —*about 1985 Tampa Bay Bandits' losing five of their last six games*

HE GAVE ME A CHANCE AND HE STUCK WITH ME. I WAS AROUND THIRTY AT THE TIME, AND THEY SAY YOU CAN'T TEACH AN OLD DOG NEW TRICKS, BUT HE COMPLETELY REVAMPED MY STYLE OF THROWING.[31]
> —**John Reaves**, *former Bandits quarterback, after Spurrier pulled him away from a real estate career and back into pro football*

He's been an outstanding player, don't get me wrong, but he hasn't played much this year and he's not gonna play for us again as long as I'm here. If they run me off, they can bring him back, I guess.[32]
> —*after releasing Bandits receiver Eric Trvillion for his alleged bad attitude*

We were 1-1 against Lee Corso. Yeah, he beat us once. Now, that is embarrassing. That's a low point, right there.[33]
> —*on his .500 record against Corso, who coached the Orlando Renegades*

Personally, I wouldn't trade Gary Anderson for Herschel Walker. Gary is the best all-around running back in the league.[34]

—on Bandits running back Gary Anderson

It's sort of like having a friend with a serious illness and he finally passed away.[35]

—after the USFL's decision not to play the 1986 season

That's the only season that I have a blank on my resume. By the time it happened, everyone was set, so I just played golf.[36]

—about not working in 1986 after the USFL folded

JOB FLIRTATIONS

Nobody has ever offered me a deal I couldn't refuse, let's put it that way. And I don't know that they will. I've got a good feeling that I could most likely refuse about any of them.[37]

I think all of us in any profession have to leave a little room for whatever. None of you (reporters) have said, "This is the only paper I'll ever work for the rest of my life." So you keep whatever options you have. If someday they get tired of me at Florida, they can get rid of me and get a better coach. If someday I don't like what's happening there, I can leave, too. It's a two-way street. That's the way all jobs are.[38]

COACHING LONGEVITY

I don't plan to coach past sixty. But it's like my little boy, Scotty, said, "Pop, what would you do? You can't play golf every day, can't lay on the beach or jump in the river every day." He's right. If I'm in good health and it's still a lot of fun, I may continue it.[39]

I think I've got some longevity. This job doesn't eat on me the way it does other coaches. I have a whole lot of other interests, like my family, playing golf, and good friends. That gives me a chance to last a long time.[40]

I DON'T THINK MONEY WAS THE DEAL IN GOING TO THE NFL. I THINK HE HAD ALL THOSE YEARS IN COLLEGE COACHING AND THAT WAS ENOUGH. HE FELT IT WAS TIME TO TRY A CHANGE. I THINK HE'LL PROBABLY RETIRE IN ABOUT EIGHT YEARS.

—*Marjorie Spurrier*, Steve's mother

Blue Devils to Gators

DUKE

There's a lot of advantages to coaching in this (Duke) environment. You don't have to worry about your players being in trouble or flunking out of school.[1]

It's going to be a challenge. People say I can't win here, but I say, "Why not?" Anything less than a winning season is not acceptable. Our goal is to make them just as excited about football as they are about basketball.[2]

One of my great football memories.[3]

—Duke's 21-17 upset of Clemson in 1989

⌒

We had a five-year reunion of the '89 Duke team back in '94, and, of course, the guys talked about this game and that game. These are memories of a lifetime when you win a championship.[4]

⌒

When Red Wilson hired me as offensive coordinator (in 1980), he told me the offense was all mine. Not many offensive coordinators, maybe not any, have that much freedom. He gave me the freedom to do what I wanted.[5]

⌒

I knew at Duke University we were not going to win games if I tried to outcoach everybody else while using the same offense all other teams used. Our personnel was not better than our opponents, and, in many instances, it was not as good. We had to come up with different plays that would give our players a chance to be successful. I think every coach in America would benefit from coaching at a school that's the underdog most of the time.[6]

⌒

Hopefully, we sold some tickets with that first play.[7]

*—about running a flea-flicker for three yards
in Duke's 1987 season-opening win over Colgate*

⌐⌐

HE WAS REALLY SOMETHING EVEN THEN, CHANGING THE WAY THAT
WHOLE TEAM PLAYED. I'M INFATUATED WITH STEVE SPURRIER. I GET
MAD AT HIM SOMETIMES, BUT I'M INFATUATED WITH HIM. WHEN HE
WAS STILL AT DUKE, I'D CALL HIM TO GET SOME PLAYS. WE WERE
COPYING HIS STUFF THEN.[8]

—Bobby Bowden, *Florida State coach*

⌐⌐

My (future job) situation can wait. Right now, it's the
Blue Devils' time to howl. I'm going to enjoy this, and
later on, we'll see if there's an opportunity that can tempt
me to leave.[9]

*—after Duke clinched a share of its first ACC title in
twenty-seven years with a 41-0 win over North Carolina*

⌐⌐

There's no better school anywhere. Durham is a wonderful place to live. Look everywhere at Duke, from faculty to students to the alumni, and you find great people. Twice, when I've had no job, Duke has hired me as a coach. This place means a great deal to Steve Spurrier and his family.[10]

This is the best feeling I've ever known as a player or coach. Team championships are much more important to me than individual awards because you got so many people to share it with.[11]

—after Duke beat North Carolina, 41-0, to win the 1989 ACC title

HE HAD AN ITCH THAT NEEDED TO BE SCRATCHED. THE FACT THAT HIS ALMA MATER WAS NOW CALLING HIM PUT HIM IN A POSITION WHERE HE HAD NO CHOICE BUT TO ACCEPT IT. AS MUCH AS I HATED TO SEE HIM LEAVE DUKE, I WAS REAL HAPPY FOR HIM.[12]

*—**Tom Butters**, former Duke athletic director*

FLORIDA GATORS

I really get excited at the games when they play the alma mater. When the band plays, "We are the boys from old Florida," it just sends chill bumps all over me.[13]

Just because I'm at my alma mater doesn't mean I'm automatically going to win. I realize I'm not going to make everybody happy.[14]

—upon taking the Florida job

When I was playing, I never thought something might not work. I was afraid if I showed any kind of doubt, the other players wouldn't believe. So even though I know I could fail here—that I could get fired—I don't think about it because I'm the coach and I can't have any doubts. Win or lose here, I'll always have fond memories of my playing days.[15]

HE WILL GO TO FLORIDA AS A WHITE KNIGHT.[16]

—*Gene Corrigan*, *former ACC commissioner*

⌒

Florida is obviously a school that means a lot to me and to my family. If the right person runs the Gators' football program correctly, they should be very successful. I'd like to think the reason they're interested in me is what I've done as a coach, and not because I went to school there and was a football hero who won the Heisman Trophy.[17]

⌒

The perfect coach for the University of Florida is maybe not a guy like me. It would be easier for one who takes all the shots and says nothing. Many coaches have it in their overall plan to get along nice and easy with the media, no matter what it takes. But it's not my way.[18]

⌒

The Swamp is where Gators live. We feel comfortable there, but we hope our opponents feel tentative. A swamp is hot and sticky and can be dangerous. We feel like this is an appropriate nickname for our stadium.[19]

—about why he nicknamed Florida Field "the Swamp"

Vince Lombardi said it best when he said winning is a habit. Teams that get used to winning will continue to win in pressure situations. And losing can be a habit, too. And there was no question from Florida's past that the university was used to losing down the stretch.[20]

It's fun coaching at Florida. All the gold in Fort Knox couldn't get me to go to the NFL.[21]

I'll live the same way I did when I was an assistant at Florida making $26,000 a year. If money were my god in life, I'd be coaching in the NFL now.[22]

—in 1997 after being given a contract extension by Florida that paid him $2 million a year

"It's fun coaching at Florida. All the gold in Fort Knox couldn't get me to go to the NFL." (Photo courtesy of University of Florida sports information office)

The real problems (at Florida) were back in 1984. That's when Florida was known as a cheating school. This thing with (former coach) Galen Hall (admitting to three NCAA violations) wasn't nearly as severe. But since it wasn't cleaned up completely, that (cheating) label is still there.[23]

That is probably the most important game our coaching staff has had here and it was the start of all the championships we've been fortunate enough to win.[24]

—*about Florida's rallying to beat Alabama, 17-13, in 1990*

DANNY WUERFFEL

I know NFL people don't think Danny Wuerffel can play, but they weren't where I was the four years he played at Florida. He's still the highest-rated quarterback in the history of college football. We won four SEC championships and a national championship with him there. It's difficult for me to believe he can't play.[25]

When he warms up before the game, sometimes he's not all that impressive. But when the game starts, that's when he's at his best.

⌒

The negative people say, Why hasn't Danny made it in the NFL? I don't have the answer for that. But tell me, at New Orleans, what quarterback did make it when he was there?

⌒

I think he's sort of like a New Testament guy. He gets slapped upside the face, and he turns the other cheek. He says: "Lord, forgive them, for they know not what they do." I'm probably more of an Old Testament guy. You spear our guy in the ear hole, and we think we're supposed to be able to spear you in the ear hole. That's how we're a little different.

—in alleging FSU was hitting Wuerffel late during the Gators' 1996 regular-season loss to the Seminoles

⌒

He's just too nice a guy, just way too nice. I've been telling him that I'm trying to relieve him of all these autograph requests and things. I tell Danny he's just got to learn to say no, but he won't do it. I can be a jerk. He can never be a jerk.[26]

RON ZOOK, HIS SUCCESSOR AT FLORIDA

I think Ron Zook is maybe better for Florida than if I was still there. I really think Ron brings energy and passion and a gung-ho for football. I think he'll do well. The Gators will embrace him eventually as a guy who loves our school.[27]

He told me I'm a tough act to follow. I told him that's why he got hired. Some of those guys who had really great jobs, they didn't want to touch it. I have a renewed excitement. Ron Zook has a renewed excitement. I think this change is better for everybody.[28]

Opponents, Rivalries, and Smirks

GEORGIA BULLDOGS

Not long after I was named head coach at Florida, several Gator fans, boosters, and others came to me and repeated what was on far too many minds: We need to quit playing Georgia in Jacksonville. We just can't beat them there, and we need to go home-and-home with them to give us a fifty-fifty chance to win. I already had thought about this great series and concluded: Why wouldn't it be an advantage for us to play Georgia in our state in a stadium named the Gator Bowl? Heck, we are the Gators.[1]

~

If we were fortunate enough to beat them ten years in a row, we'd want to beat them just as bad in the eleventh as we did in the first.[2]

⌒

I'M SURE (SPURRIER) WILL GIVE US PLENTY OF MATERIAL FOR THE BULLETIN BOARD.[3]

—Alec Millen, former Georgia tackle

⌒

Ray (Goff, former Georgia coach) and I aren't buddy-buddy or anything like that. Some coaches can be friends with coaches they go up against all the time, but I'm not that way.[4]

⌒

Why is it that during recruiting season they sign all the great players, but when it comes time to play the game, we have all the great players? I don't understand that. What happens to them?

—from postgame news conference after beating Georgia, 45-13, in 1991, addressing what he felt was poor-mouthing by Georgia in previous years prior to the Florida-Georgia game

⌒

I wasn't bragging about outcoaching Ray Goff. That's just Georgia people looking for something nasty and negative about me and the Gators. It's the nature of the rivalry.[5]

TRUTH IS, THE GATOR BOWL DOESN'T HOLD ALL THE ADVANTAGES FOR GEORGIA THAT IT USED TO. FOR A SPAN OF TWO DECADES (1970–89), JUST THE THOUGHT OF ENTERING THAT PLACE USED TO FREEZE GATOR BLOOD. THAT'S ALL SHATTERED NOW. THE COMING OF STEVE SPURRIER AND HIS BAGGAGE CARS FULL OF EGO CHANGED EVERYTHING.[6]

*—**Steve Hummer**, Atlanta Constitution columnist*

We knew coming in nobody had scored fifty against them here, so that's what we wanted to do. This may be the only time in our lifetime that Florida plays here, so we wanted to make it memorable for the Gators.[7]

—on why he had no regrets about scoring a late touchdown in 1995 to beat Georgia, 52-17, in Athens

A familiar scene at Florida during Spurrier's twelve seasons coaching there. (Photo courtesy of University of Florida sports information office)

FLORIDA STATE

You know what FSU stands for, don't you? Free Shoes University.

—addressing Polk County Gator booster club in 1994 after Florida State's Foot Locker scandal

I DON'T LET IT BOTHER ME. AFTER ALL, THE SHOES WERE FREE, BUT WE PAID A HECK OF A PRICE FOR IT.[8]

—**Bobby Bowden**, *responding to Spurrier's bringing up the joke again*

Bobby Bowden tells his little Gator jokes and we tell our little Seminole jokes. That's been going on for years. I have no hard feelings when they tell jokes about us. I'm not one of those guys who's always giving it out and can't take it.

FSU has to have the best recruiters in college football. The way they can convince these players that they can go up there and beat out the high school All-Americans that are already there. I don't know how they do it, but you've got to give them credit.[9]

I guess I'm supposed to cry a lot because that's what FSU people say I do. I'm not really much of a crier. I don't get all choked up. I don't understand why they said I was crying. I guess because we only won by twenty-four that day (referring to Florida's 37-13 win over FSU in November 2001).[10]

—on not being emotional during his farewell news conference at Florida

They came back and tied us and then beat us in the Sugar Bowl, so we got about what we deserved, not holding a twenty-eight-point lead.[11]

—about blowing a 31-3 lead against
FSU in 1994, then losing the bowl rematch

I wonder if (Bobby Bowden) instructs this type of action. I've had enough, and sometimes someone has to speak out. Everyone in college football knows this kind of crap should not happen. And it happens over and over when we play these guys. We've got all the video on it. I'm not making this stuff up.

—alleging that Florida State's Darnell Dockett
twisted the knee of UF tailback Earnest Graham
on purpose in the Gators' 37-13 win over FSU in November 2001

Certainly I'm not taking anything back. The way they hit
Wuerffel wasn't right. The reason it didn't happen again
in the Sugar Bowl is because the head referee controlled
the game.[12]

—alleging that FSU made late hits on quarterback
Danny Wuerffel in 1996 regular-season loss to Seminoles

MIAMI HURRICANES

We can't hide, duck, or blink when the University of
Miami is mentioned. We need to play Miami. I'm not saying we're going to beat Miami. They might beat us, 50-0.
But if our goal is to be as good as they've been, obviously
we need to play them. In the WAC (Western Athletic
Conference), they play twelve games a year because one is
outside the continental United States. If Miami wants, we
can go play somewhere in the Bahamas next year.[13]

—from his first news conference as Florida's new
coach, on why the Gators should resume playing Miami

DALLAS COWBOYS

I can't make any guarantees, but we will be ready to play the Dallas Cowboys.[14]

—from his first news conference as Washington Redskins head coach

Hopefully, our Georgia.[15]

—upon being asked if the Cowboys were going to be his NFL version of Florida State

They've beaten us nine in a row, did you know that? They sort of got our number. All I'm saying is we need to beat those guys. We've got no excuses. When somebody is beating you like that, you got to step up and do something. The Cowboys are even beating us in their down years. We need to address that.

POKING FUN AT OPPONENTS

I guess they had some extra money. I guess they used some
of that Pell Grant money.[16]

> *—after learning that the University of Miami, which*
> *was under investigation for misuse of Pell Grant*
> *funds, had a larger football promotional poster than Florida's*

~

I don't see why. I've won more games on that field than
he has.

> *—after learning that North Carolina coach Mack Brown was angry*
> *that Spurrier brought his Duke players back on the field to*
> *have a team picture taken underneath the scoreboard*
> *following a 41-0 Duke victory to clinch the 1989 ACC title*

~

But the real tragedy was that fifteen hadn't been colored yet.

> *—referring to an Auburn dormitory fire that destroyed twenty books*

~

You can't spell Citrus without U-T.

*—on Tennessee's frequent appearance
in the Citrus Bowl in the mid-1990s*

I'm not saying anybody broke any rules; I'm just saying there was a feeling of, well, those kids are driving awfully nice cars. How's it happen?[17]

*—talking about how nice the cars looked
in the Florida State players' parking lot*

Their pass defense was No. 1 in the nation coming in, but it won't be going out.

—after UF handed Mississippi State a 52-0 loss in 2001

If I had a defense like Hal Mumme has, I'd be trying them on every kickoff.

—after Kentucky tried several onside kicks during Florida's 1997 victory

We should have beat them like that. We knew they weren't very good.

*—following a 50-7 win over
Oklahoma State in his first game as Florida's coach*

Quarterbacks and Pitching It Around

QUARTERBACKS

I'm a quarterback coach of fundamentals. There's a right way and a wrong way to throw a pass. There's a right way and a wrong way to hold the ball, shift your weight, position your head to look off a receiver. It's like a golf swing. You know all those little flaws in a golf swing that we all have? Well, quarterbacks can have those, also.[1]

"I'm a quarterback coach of fundamentals. There's a right way and a wrong way to throw a pass." Here, a young Spurrier gives a demonstration as the Gators' quarterback. (Photo courtesy of University of Florida sports information office)

A quarterback's got to make good decisions. One thing we do that's probably a lot different than what I've been watching is our quarterbacks audible. We check off. We change the play.

—from his introductory news conference as Redskins coach

Just like Tiger Woods has a golf coach, there is going to be a guy coaching these quarterbacks, too. If other NFL coaches don't want to coach their quarterbacks, that's OK.[2]

I know you have to have a quarterback, but I also know backups have won the last two Super Bowls.[3]

I don't know who the quarterback will be. But he'll lead the league in passing.

—speaking to a Gator booster club before his first season at Florida

Beauty is in the eye of the beholder. A lot of my guys haven't been the six-four, six-five quarterbacks others like. I'll use the six-one guy.[4]

~

Over the years, people have insisted that our quarterbacks are all products of the offensive system, but that is far from correct. It takes the right kind of quarterback to operate the system properly because he is so involved in the on-field choices in reacting to the various defensive alignments.[5]

~

I just don't want to do any zigzagging during games. I don't want a guy to feel like with one or two interceptions, he's out of there.[6]

~

I FEEL AFTER I GRADUATE, NO MATTER WHO THE QUARTERBACK IS AT FLORIDA, HE'LL PUT UP BIG NUMBERS BECAUSE OF THE SYSTEM. COACH SPURRIER IS SIMPLY A GREAT TEACHER.[7]

—*Shane Matthews*, *former Florida quarterback*

~

COACH SPURRIER CAN STAND ON THE SIDELINES, WITH OR WITH-
OUT A HEADSET, AND LOOK AT THE DEFENSE, AND 95 PERCENT OF
THE TIME HE'LL PICK A PLAY THAT'S GOING TO WORK FOR US. THE
WAY HE SEES THE WHOLE FIELD IS AMAZING.[8]

—*Brian Schottenheimer*, *former Florida quarterback*

I REMEMBER BEING MORE NERVOUS AT PRACTICE THAN GAMES
BECAUSE DEFENSES DIDN'T APPLY THE PRESSURE HE DID. YOU CAN
GO TWO WAYS WITH HIM: YOU CAN QUIT OR YOU CAN PROVE HIM
WRONG.[9]

—*Dave Brown*, *former Duke quarterback*

HIS QUARTERBACK IS HIM ON THE FIELD.[10]

—*Steve Slayden*, *former Duke quarterback*

The quarterback must be intelligent and poised under pressure. That is more important than pure physical ability. We
try to give a lot of freedom to the quarterback and with
that comes the responsibility for him to make good choices
and not make the crucial mistakes that beat you.[11]

I believe that throwing the football is a very natural motion, and that a three-quarters overhand delivery, the same way a baseball pitcher throws a fastball, is best.[12]

One thing I'll never do is be critical of a quarterback. I've thrown to the wrong place myself a lot of times, and I know you don't need the coach making you feel any worse.[13]

Nah, you've been reading these other sportswriters too much. I don't jerk quarterbacks around.[14]

—dismissing speculation that he would pull
Danny Wuerffel after three interceptions against LSU

HE GETS INTO YOUR HEAD. HE TESTS YOU AT PRACTICE 'TIL YOU ALMOST BREAK. IF YOU COULD HANDLE THAT, GAME DAY WAS EASY.[15]

*—**Anthony Dilweg**, former Duke quarterback*

The quarterback who doesn't make it, who does he blame? He blames me.[16]

MASTERING SPURRIER'S OFFENSE

WHEN I FIRST TOOK IT OVER, IT SEEMED LIKE I WAS TRYING TO TRANSLATE WAR AND PEACE ONTO THE FOOTBALL FIELD.[17]

—**Ben Bennett**, *former Duke quarterback*

WITH ALL HE IS ABLE TO DO, YOU DON'T NEED A GREAT ARM TO THROW IN THAT OFFENSE. YOU LOOK AND PEOPLE ARE WIDE OPEN.[18]

—**Billy Ray**, *former Duke quarterback*

EVERY TIME I LOOK OVER AT COACH, YOU CAN SEE THE WHEELS SPINNING. BUT YOU KNOW WHAT? THERE'S STILL ABOUT A THOU-SAND PLAYS I NEVER CALLED. WE GOT MORE PLAYS THAN FLORIDA HAS SAND.[19]

—*Danny Wuerffel*, *after Florida beat Alabama for the SEC Championship*

HIS WHOLE OFFENSE IS BASED ON TIMING. NOBODY ELSE CAN RUN (HIS OFFENSIVE SYSTEM). EVERY SINGLE PLAY, HE DESIGNED. I CAN REMEMBER TIMES WE'D GO TO THE SIDELINE AND HE'D MAKE UP A PLAY IN FIVE OR SIX SECONDS.[20]

—*Travis Taylor*, *former Florida receiver now with the Baltimore Ravens*

THE NFL LORDS WILL PROBABLY STRIKE ME DEAD, BUT STEVE SPURRIER KNOWS MORE ABOUT OFFENSIVE FOOTBALL THAN ANY OF THEM EVER THOUGHT ABOUT KNOWING. I DIDN'T KNOW ANY-THING ABOUT PLAYING QUARTERBACK UNTIL I PLAYED UNDER STEVE IN THE USFL. HE TAUGHT ME MORE ABOUT MECHANICS, UNDERSTANDING COVERAGES, AND THE THEORY BEHIND THE PASSING GAME THAN ANY COACH I HAD IN THE NFL.[21]

—*John Reaves*, *former Florida assistant coach, speaking in 1990*

A LOT OF TEAMS CAN PASS THE BALL AND NOT REALLY ATTACK THAT HARD. THERE'S A LOT OF SAFE ROUTES. SPURRIER UNDERSTANDS THE SHORT GAME, WHAT TO DO IN THE RED ZONE, HOW TO HANDLE MAN AND ZONE COVERAGES. HE'S GOT A GREAT FEEL FOR WHAT TO DO WHEN A DEFENSE DOES A CERTAIN THING. IF YOU PLAY JUST TWO-DEEP AND THREE-DEEP OR MAN COVERAGE, HE WILL KILL YOU. YOU BETTER DO SOMETHING TO CONFUSE HIM. HE'S THE BEST OFFENSIVE COACH THAT COLLEGE FOOTBALL HAS SEEN IN A LONG TIME.[22]

—**Mark Richt**, *Georgia coach*

THE WAY (SPURRIER) SEES IT, IF WE DON'T GAIN AT LEAST FOUR HUNDRED YARDS, IT LOOKS BAD ON HIM.[23]

—**Billy Ray**, *former Duke quarterback*

PHILOSOPHY

I read somewhere that to be successful in life, you've got to outwork the competition, or else you have to do things differently. Maybe I'm just trying to do things a little different.[24]

To me, a good offense is one that looks complicated, but is simple to learn and teach the players.[25]

⌒

Basically, there is a good pass play for every defense. There isn't any one great defense that can shut down the pass or everybody would be using it.[26]

⌒

THERE'S NOBODY WHO PREPARES HIS TEAM MORE FOR THE PASS-ING GAME THAN SPURRIER. THE NUMBERS DON'T LIE. A LOT OF DEFENSIVE COACHES IN COLLEGE FOOTBALL ARE TRYING TO SOLVE THE PROBLEMS THAT HIS OFFENSE CREATES—AND THEY DON'T DO IT VERY OFTEN.[27]

—*Marty Schottenheimer,* Spurrier's
head-coaching predecessor with the Redskins

⌒

Coaches say the running game opens up the passing game. I don't see why you can't open up the running game by passing. You don't have to run first. You've got to do both, but not in any order.[28]

⌒

My favorite coach of all time is John Wooden, without question. A friend of mine sent me a taped radio interview with him, and I've picked off a bunch of his philosophies and ideas about coaching. I go over it with our team once or twice a year. I think he was a guy that coached the best way of anybody that I've ever heard talk about the game.[29]

In the big picture, we strive to have a balanced offense, but we don't go out each week and say we need to run it 50 percent of the time and pass it 50 percent. Depending on the defense we are facing, it could be heavily slanted toward either running or passing in any particular game. We're basically going to be an attacking offense for the entire game—no matter the score. If we're way ahead, we still will put it in the air because that's our game.[30]

If your players are not performing at a level that you expect them to, then you've got to try the next player. That's my philosophy. You try to consistently have competition for positions.[31]

The NFL and
the Redskins

$25 MILLION CONTRACT

Well, the size of my contract has been too big for the last
ten years anyway. I just sort of know the money's a lot bigger than it used to be everywhere. Coaches are making
more. Players are making more. I will certainly try to give
to the charities in this area and be involved. I believe in
life if you're fortunate enough to make a little extra, you
should share it.

—from his introductory press conference as Redskins coach

COACHING THE REDSKINS

It was the opportunity to coach on the national scene for a team that plays in the largest stadium in the National Football League, that sells all those tickets and with all those fans. They're the best fans in the NFL. It's so loud there.[1]

If I was ever going to coach in the NFL, this is it. It's time to see if my style of coaching, my kind of offense can work in that league. I'd like to coach five or six more years and see what happens. If it doesn't work out, I'll just be a retired ball coach.[2]

After I talked to Dan Snyder, we basically did the deal that night and I was all set. I've lived in Florida thirty-one of the last thirty-seven years and I sort of felt like, let's get out of Florida for five or six years and see if we can make it happen on a very big stage in D.C.

—on not having regrets about accepting the job before the Tampa Bay Buccaneers post came open

HE IS THE HEAD COACH OF THE REDSKINS FOR FIVE YEARS, AT A MINIMUM. I'VE STAKED MY CREDIBILITY—ALONG WITH HIS—TOGETHER. I HOPE WE HAVE A SUCCESSFUL SEASON. I THINK AND PRAY THAT WE WILL. BUT IF WE DON'T, I WILL STAND BY COACH SPURRIER FOR HOWEVER LONG IT TAKES BECAUSE HE WILL GET IT RIGHT. HE'S A WINNER.[3]

—**Dan Snyder**, *Washington Redskins owner*

EVERYBODY IN AMERICA'S GOING TO BE WATCHING THE REDSKINS, AND THEY'RE HOPING WE'RE GOING TO FAIL. BUT WE'RE GOING TO PROVE THEM WRONG.[4]

—**Shane Matthews**, *another former Gator quarterback reunited with Spurrier with the Redskins*

I think it's all very similar to what we see in college. There's not a whole bunch of new defenses out there. Obviously, the pros play better, and they're better athletes, but it looks about the same. We pitched it around in the USFL (1983–85). We pitched it around at Duke (1987–89). We pitched it around at Florida. I came here to see if we can pitch it around in the NFL. I don't see why we can't.[5]

We think we've got a good enough team to win the (NFC East) division. Shoot, there's only three other teams in the division. It's not like trying to win the SEC.

—assessing the 2002 season

It's always of interest to me that people say, "His receivers in college were mostly wide open, but in the NFL they won't be." Well, we'll find out. It intrigues me to see if we can do that.[6]

HE'LL LEAD THE LEAGUE IN OFFENSE OR BE CLOSE TO IT. FOLD ME UP AND SEND ME TO RUSSIA IF IT DOESN'T HAPPEN.[7]

*—**John Reaves**, who coached under Spurrier at Florida and played for him with the USFL Tampa Bandits*

IT LOOKS LIKE A RECIPE FOR DISASTER, FILLING YOUR ROSTER WITH
HOMERS, BUT TAKE A LOOK AT WHAT JIMMY JOHNSON DID WHEN
HE GOT TO DALLAS. I'M GUESSING THAT SPURRIER HAS A FEEL FOR
WHAT HE'S DOING. OFFENSIVELY, EVERYBODY KNOWS HE'S GOT A
SPECIAL GIFT. HE'LL ACCLIMATE. JUST WATCH.[8]

—*Jerry Angelo*, Chicago Bears general manager

It wears on you. We were double-digit favorites over everybody, and any time we'd lose, it was us coaches (to blame).
We screwed up. I'd kind of like to be the underdog again.

—*from his farewell news conference at Florida*

TO BE HONEST—AND HE'S NOT GOING TO LIKE THIS—I THINK
HE'S HAVING A BIT OF A MIDDLE-AGED CRISIS, AND INSTEAD OF
BUYING A SPORTS CAR OR GETTING A TROPHY WIFE, HE WENT OFF
TO THE NFL, WHICH I GUESS IS MUCH SAFER. HE'S GOT AN ITCH,
AND HE WANTS TO SCRATCH IT.[9]

—*Joe Biddle*, a childhood friend and Nashville Tennessean *sportswriter*

PEOPLE HAVE BEEN ASKING ME FOR FIVE YEARS, "WOULD COACH SPURRIER'S OFFENSE WORK IN THE NFL?" COACH DOESN'T HAVE AN OFFENSE. HE ADAPTS TO THE DEFENSE EVERY WEEK.[10]

—**Danny Wuerffel**, *quarterback*

SPURRIER'S GOING TO BE BIGGER THAN (MICHAEL) JORDAN IN THIS TOWN. THIS IS THE REDSKINS, AND NOTHING'S BIGGER THAN THE REDSKINS IN D.C.[11]

—**Maury Povich**, *talk-show host, a lifelong Redskins fan*

DAN SNYDER

I talked to Brian Schottenheimer. Brian said, "He's a nice guy. My dad and he just didn't get along." I've really never had any trouble working for anyone and I don't anticipate any major disagreements.

—*from the NFL owners' meetings, March 2002*

I really believe I'm here because Dan Snyder convinced me this is the best opportunity. He convinced me to be his coach.

~

He sold me by his passion and love of the team. He wants to bring a championship back to D.C.[12]

~

Someone asked if I could survive (owner) Dan Snyder. Shoot, I tell them I survived at Duke twice.

~

He won't be any tougher than the Gators. He won't be any tougher than me.

—on whether his owner will be tough to deal with after a loss

~

The first game ball I'm going to give Mr. Snyder is when we play the Dallas Cowboys.

~

I SWEAR, HE WOULD RATHER BE ON HIS OWN FIVE-YARD LINE AND GO TO THE END ZONE NINETY-FIVE YARDS AWAY THAN PUNCH IT IN FROM THREE YARDS OUT. STEVE LOVES A LITTLE BIT OF THE UNDERDOG THING. MR. SNYDER OFFERED HIM A CHALLENGE. THAT'S ALL HE NEEDED TO HEAR.[13]

—*Ray Graves*, *former Florida coach*

REDSKINS' FUTURE

I know people are wondering about how I am going to make the adjustment from college to the pros, but our offense will finish ranked in the top five in the league. You can count on that.[14]

Most coaches have assistant coaches with them that they've been with. If they can collect players that have been with them before, they do that. That's just human nature. But I assure you that if they're not the best players, they will not play.

—*on signing so many former Florida players*

MARVIN LEWIS, REDSKINS' DEFENSIVE COORDINATOR

I'm a big believer that Marvin's worth around a million bucks a year. If you pay your left guard or your backup linebacker a million bucks, why wouldn't your defensive coordinator make a million bucks?

NFL SCHEME

Sometimes our linemen say, "Coach, we've got too many protections." But our scheme has held up for about eighteen years. It's not the first time I've been a head coach. The scheme has held up over a period of time, or else we've just been very lucky to score so many points and lead the conference, lead the nation in total offense. I don't think you're giving the college defensive guys much credit to think it's a whole bunch different game. But only time will tell. We'll let it play out and go from there.[15]

ON CHANGING HIS COACHING STYLE FOR THE NFL

I think every head coach has to do it their way, the way that's been successful for them and what they believe in. I was hearing Jimmy Johnson talk about maybe the best way was for the head coach to work hand in hand with the general manager and the personnel staff. We try to do that. I'm the type of coach who feels like maybe what I do best is coach the offense and hopefully, we've got excellent personnel people to help put the players in place.[16]

2002 NFL DRAFT, HIS FIRST

On drafting quarterback Patrick Ramsey:
We think he's got a chance to be a really fine young player. He's really smart. We'll bring him in and let him compete with the guys we have here. We think he has a really strong arm. He can make all the throws.[17]

I'm involved in the draft about the same way I was in (college) recruiting. I check out the quarterbacks and receivers and between the owner and personnel people, we decide who we want to draft. This is not my team. This is our team.

JOE GIBBS

I hope when my time is finished here, my departure will be similar to Joe Gibbs. Not many coaches walk out on their own terms.[18]

REDSKINS' COLOR SCHEME

We're burgundy (and gold). That other school (Florida State) is not burgundy. We're okay.[19]

BEING THE OFFENSIVE COORDINATOR

Why do I do it? Because that's what I did before I was ever a head coach. So why should I let someone else run the offense when I know I can do it?[20]

Sometimes people think all (I do) is throw it all over the ballpark. But we're going to run the ball, too.[21]

When you're the head coach, offensive coordinator, and quarterback coach, you can call any dadgum play you want.[22]

"I don't think telling the truth ever gets anyone in trouble in the long run. Maybe the day after, but not in the long run." (Photo courtesy of University of Florida sports information office)

Spurrier
His Own Self

SPEAKING HIS MIND

I'm not one to say "no comment" whether I'm
right or wrong, but especially if I'm right.[1]

⁓

I don't think telling the truth ever gets anyone in
trouble in the long run. Maybe the day after, but
not in the long run.[2]

⁓

As long as people are fair with me, then we have a great relationship, a wonderful relationship. But when a few of them write lies and lies and lies, then I just end that relationship and they're on the outside.[3]

Lou (Holtz) was lucky as hell and he knows it. His defense wasn't very good. It certainly wasn't that night. But we couldn't capitalize. We kept kicking field goals instead of taking it on in.[4]

—responding to suggestions that Notre Dame's Lou Holtz outcoached him in the 1992 Sugar Bowl that Florida lost, 39-28

That guy who said defense wins championships hasn't watched us a lot.[5]

We wish him well, but field goals have never been too important to us.[6]

—about losing Parade All-America kicker T. J. Tucker to professional baseball

There are people out there who're against me. They'll call me paranoid, but some of the loudest critics see us as being the big school down here; the one that's supposed to have all the athletes. Some people don't like seeing us get it together, having good seasons and winning SEC championships. But I can live with that. I'll kiss no fannies to get good reviews.[7]

I don't really think I say all that much. It just gets interpreted stronger, I guess, because no other coaches say anything. Don't you think that's part of it?

STEVE'S A BRAT. HE DOESN'T TAKE EVERYTHING IN THIS WORLD SO SERIOUSLY. SARCASM, TEASING, DIGGING: HE LOVES THAT KIND OF STUFF. HE'S GREAT AT IT.[8]

—*Jerri Spurrier*

All that negative stuff, you know what that is? That's what losers do. They try to find chinks in your armor.[9]

—*responding to criticism that his Florida team didn't deserve the No. 1 preseason ranking in 2001*

HE SAYS THINGS A LOT OF US THINK, BUT DON'T HAVE GUTS
ENOUGH TO SAY.[10]

—*Bobby Bowden*

⌒

HE'LL SAY THINGS, AND EVEN IF YOU'RE SENSITIVE ABOUT IT,
YOU'LL KNOW EXACTLY WHAT HE MEANT TO SAY. FOR ME, THE
OLDER I GOT, THE MORE I UNDERSTOOD HIM. AS AN ADULT, YOU
CAN TELL IT'S CONSTRUCTIVE. IT'S PROBABLY BOTH HIS BEST AND
WORST QUALITY, BUT IF YOU LET IT, IT CAN REALLY HELP YOU.[11]

—*daughter* **Lisa**

⌒

LISA AND I HAD AN UNWRITTEN RULE WHEN WE WERE KIDS, THAT
WE WEREN'T GOING TO DO ANYTHING MY DAD COULD COACH US
IN. RUNNING, JUMPING ROPE. HE ALWAYS KNEW A BETTER WAY, A
MORE EFFICIENT WAY TO DO IT. AND HE'D TELL YOU ABOUT IT.[12]

—*daughter* **Amy**

⌒

A bunch of history professors.

*—expressing his displeasure with the NCAA Committee
on Infractions after it ruled Florida ineligible for a 1990 bowl game*

⌒

They wouldn't contact me. You (media) guys got them
convinced I can't win in domes and I can't win on
Astroturf.[13]

*—on why the Atlanta Falcons failed
to approach him about their coaching vacancy*

⌒

Our annual team picture.[14]

*—while his team posed on the field after
winning its third consecutive Southeastern Conference title*

⌒

STEVE'S A GREAT COACH. . . . BUT HE JUST CAN'T SHUT UP.[15]

—Dennis Erickson, former Miami coach

⌒

Can't you find another word? I don't know. How 'bout mastermind?

—asking a North Carolina sportswriter when he was the Duke coach to stop referring to him as an offensive genius

IT DOESN'T BOTHER ME WHAT PEOPLE MIGHT SAY ABOUT HIM. I KNOW STEVE ISN'T GUILTY OF A LOT OF THINGS HE'S ACCUSED OF. HIS DAD AND I NEVER TRIED TO CORRECT HIM ON THINGS HE'S SAID OR DONE.

*—**Marjorie Spurrier**, Steve's mother*

ARROGANCE

That's fine—people can call me arrogant, cocky, whatever. At least they're not calling us losers anymore. If people like you too much, it's probably because they're beating you.[16]

WHAT DO THEY BASE THAT ON? BECAUSE HE'S A FIERY COACH ON THE SIDELINE AND HE WINS CHAMPIONSHIPS? BECAUSE HE DOES IT THE RIGHT WAY? HIS TEAMS HAVE NEVER BEEN ACCUSED OF DOING ANYTHING WRONG, AND FROM HAVING WORKED WITH HIM, I CAN SAY THAT EVERYTHING HE DOES IS BY THE BOOK. HIS CODE OF ETHICS IS UNQUESTIONABLE. HE'S A MUCH MORE APPRECIATIVE AND GRATEFUL PERSON THAN I BELIEVE HE'S EVER GIVEN CREDIT FOR.[17]

—Bob Stoops, *Oklahoma coach*

IF YOU LOOK AT A BASKETBALL COACH, HE'S UP AND HOLLERING AND YELLING AT OFFICIALS AND GETTING AFTER PLAYERS, BUT NOBODY EVER SAYS ANYTHING BAD ABOUT A BASKETBALL COACH BECAUSE WE THINK THEY'RE SUPPOSED TO COACH LIKE THAT. BUT STEVE'S THE SAME WAY. HE'S HIGHLY INVOLVED, HE'S WORKING THE SIDELINES, HE'S VERY DEMONSTRATIVE. THAT'S JUST HIS STYLE. SOME PEOPLE TAKE OFFENSE TO THAT STYLE. BUT THAT DOESN'T MAKE HIM A BAD PERSON.[18]

—Jeremy Foley, *Florida athletic director*

STEVE SPURRIER REMAINS THE SMARTEST MAN WHO EVER LIVED. IF YOU DON'T BELIEVE ME, JUST ASK HIM.[19]

—Mark Bradley, *columnist for the* Atlanta Journal and Constitution

PEOPLE SAY HE'S ARROGANT, BUT IT'S ALL ABOUT SELF-
CONFIDENCE. HE TAKES PRESSURE OFF HIS TEAM BY PUTTING
A BIG BULL'S-EYE ON HIS BACK THAT SAYS, "COME AND GET ME!"
THE GUY'S A SWASHBUCKLER.[20]

—*Danny Sheridan*, *college football analyst*

HE PROBABLY THINKS HE'S A GURU, THINKS HE'S SOME OFFENSIVE
WIZARD. AND THAT REALLY PISSES SOME PEOPLE OFF.[21]

—*Johnny Majors*, *former Pittsburgh/Tennessee coach*

I DON'T LOOK AT HIM AS OVERLY ARROGANT. MAYBE
EGOMANIACAL.[22]

—*Terry Dean*, *former Florida quarterback*

COACHING STYLE

Some people have mentioned that at our practices the coaches aren't constantly screaming and criticizing players. This is something I thoroughly believe: As a coach, you coach first. Your overriding priority is to teach, teach, teach. There eventually comes a point, after you have exhausted your teaching and your encouraging, where if a player is not giving the effort, not paying attention, loafing, then it is time to criticize.[23]

I'm not the kind of coach who screams and hollers at a guy. You can't do that with quarterbacks. It just makes them mad at you. You can do that with linemen who have to hit, but not quarterbacks.[24]

—prior to his first season as a college coach

TOSSING HIS VISOR

When we coach our offense, we aren't just trying to win, we're trying to play the perfect game. We want to go up and down the field and score a touchdown every time we touch the ball. When I see players—quarterbacks, receivers, linemen, whoever—not playing up to potential, that is upsetting to me. Bad plays will happen, of course, but we need to show displeasure when they occur. Some coaches can mask their emotions, but I'm just not one of them.[25]

We've got to talk to Reebok about sending a letter out to the company that makes good visors. I can't wear those little ones like Jon Gruden wears.[26]

DEMEANOR

I've got a clear conscience about the way I act.[27]

In 1991, my second year as head coach of the Gators, we put a 35-0 loss on Alabama. But then I got a letter from an old friend, a Gator fan. He says I'm too emotional. That I'd better tone it down or I would quickly burn out. Following weekend, we go to Syracuse. I'm real calm. Before I awoke, we were down 14-0. We come back, still got beat (38-21). I decided right there in the Carrier Dome that I was going to coach my fanny off all the time.[28]

HE'S ALWAYS BEEN COOL AND CALM. OF COURSE, HE GETS A LITTLE UPSET ON THE SIDELINES. MY DAD HAS A PRETTY GOOD TEMPER, BUT STEVE DIDN'T LEARN TO CONTROL IT LIKE WE DO MOST OF THE TIME. THAT'S JUST PART OF HIS COMPETITIVENESS, I BELIEVE.[29]

—*Graham Spurrier*, Steve's brother

DO YOU KNOW IN THIRTY YEARS HE'S NEVER RAISED HIS VOICE AT ME? NEVER. HE'S NOT AN EXTREME, EMOTIONAL PERSON. THE EMOTION ON THE FIELD IS THE MOST YOU'LL EVER SEE OF THAT.[30]

—*Jerri Spurrier*

CRITICISM

I got one of John Wooden's sayings on my wall. He says, "The more successful you are, the more you are criticized." So every time I get criticized, I say, "Gosh, I must be pretty successful or they wouldn't give a dang about me."[31]

When I came to Florida, critics said I had to run the ball and play defense to be successful. Until you do something, critics look for reasons to say that you can't. It makes people feel good for some reason to criticize. That's just the way life is.

Certainly, we try to encourage our players to say the right things. But they don't always do it. We don't muzzle them. We believe in free speech and if they say something bad about the coaches, we don't always kick them off the team.[32]

I get so many nice write-ups all over the country. Then there are one or two negative ones, and I'm really glad there are. I think we need some enemies out there to help keep us alert. To stir the fires. To avoid complacency.[33]

⁓

I used to get upset when people wrote negative things about me and the Gators. I really try not to respond to the critics any more. But I know who they are.[34]

⁓

Why would somebody in Alabama or Georgia, that are Bulldogs or Auburn War Eagles or Crimson Tide people, why would they want to think favorably of me?[35]

⁓

The only people that want us to do well are our fans and families. Outside people don't want us to succeed. I go back to a book Dr. Sydney Harris wrote called *Winners and Losers*. He says a winner admires and respects other winners. A loser resents winners and tries to find something negative to say about them.

⁓

One of the national guys on ESPN, *The Sports Reporters*, said Spurrier is going to be like Rick Pitino (a successful college coach who didn't fare well in the pros). I guess until we kick off, that's all fair. We'll see. The people that don't know me are going to try their best to get their criticisms in.

Alphabet Steve

AUTOGRAPHS

IT NEVER ENDS. WE GET EVERYTHING. HE AUTOGRAPHS
EVERYTHING THAT'S SENT IN. IT MAY TAKE A WHILE,
BUT HE'LL EVENTUALLY GET TO IT. I BET I SEND OUT AT
LEAST SEVENTY-FIVE TO A HUNDRED FIVE-BY-SEVEN
(AUTOGRAPHED) PHOTOS EVERY WEEK. HE'S REAL
GOOD ABOUT PERSONALIZING IF HE CAN. HE'S VERY
CONSCIOUS OF WHAT IT MEANS TO PEOPLE.[1]

—**Nancy Sain**, *Spurrier's secretary at Florida*

COMPETITIVENESS

I don't like to shake hands with the other coach after losing. To me, it's a little bit of an embarrassment. That coach has beaten you and in his mind he's saying, "I'm tougher than Spurrier. I had my team better prepared than Spurrier." That's all the motivation I need.[2]

When Nebraska took a knee at the end of the (1996) Fiesta Bowl, I wanted to call timeout and go over and tell Tom Osborne to try to score another touchdown, but I chickened out. I'm a competitor. If you have a chance to beat me, beat me as bad as you can.[3]

"If you have a chance to beat me, beat me as bad as you can."
(Photo courtesy of University of Florida sports information office)

IT DIDN'T MATTER IF WE WERE PLAYING PING-PONG OR PITCHING HORSESHOES, IT WAS ALWAYS FOR THE CHAMPIONSHIP OF THE WORLD. HE WAS THE MOST CONFIDENT PERSON I'D EVER BEEN AROUND.[4]

—*Lonnie Lowe, Spurrier's best friend as a child in Johnson City, Tennessee*

EXPECTATIONS

I want expectations to be high. I'm a firm believer that if you expect certain things to happen, then there's a good chance they will.[5]

—*going into his first season at Florida*

In this day and age, expectations and timing are everything. If I had gone 7-4, 7-4, 8-3, 8-3 to start off (at Florida), everybody would say, "Man, we're getting close." But once you get to where we are, the expectations are way up there. I don't know if we can win five of the next six SEC titles.[6]

FAITH

My profession is coaching. I leave the preaching to the ministers.[7]

~

I accepted Christ a long time ago. I'm not the best Christian in the world, I know that, but I believe in the Bible and what it says. I don't believe God cares who wins or loses, but I believe God helps those who help themselves. I'm just not as outward about it.[8]

~

FAMILY LIFE

Basically, it was her idea. The kids were in high school or college. She'd go do her aerobic workout and come home and nobody was there. So she felt the need to raise another little one.[9]

—*on the decision to adopt their youngest child, Scotty, in 1986*

~

I BENEFITED MUCH MORE THAN MY SISTERS DID. I GOT TO GO TO PRACTICE. I GOT TO GO IN THE LOCKER ROOM. I GOT TO LISTEN TO HIM TALK EVERYWHERE HE WENT. MY SISTERS COULDN'T DO THAT. THEY MISSED OUT A LOT ON THAT. AFTER SCHOOL, I COULD GO OUT TO PRACTICE AND I GOT A PIECE OF MY DAD THROUGH THAT.[10]

—*Steve Spurrier Jr.*, *Washington Redskins assistant coach*

GOLF

First, it's the toughest sport anyone could ever attempt to play. It is you against the course, and nobody else can carry the load for you if you have a poor day. Golf is fascinating. All of us think we should play better than we do.[11]

Golf relates to life. The ball is not always going to bounce your way, and the putts are not always going to drop. The true grinder who competes the hardest will generally be the winner.[12]

I played Augusta National the other day. I shot an 82.
I hit the ball real well, but my putting was off. It's not
that tough a course, but you still got to put the ball in
the hole.[13]

~

My golf game is mostly intense and serious during the off-
season. When football practice starts, I put the clubs away
and don't give the game much thought. That's probably a
lot different from the impression of those who believed the
rumor that I was a country club coach. I remember one
morning I was in the office at 5:30, and one of my assis-
tants told me I had better not let anyone know I came in
that early or it would ruin my reputation.[14]

~

I think I enjoy the game of golf so much because of the
way golfers act. People who play golf generally appreciate
things. People who play golf are not afraid to fail, they're
not afraid to make themselves look silly at times. It
teaches humility.[15]

~

HE'S VERY BIG ON TRUTH AND HONESTY. YOU
PLAY GOLF WITH HIM, YOU PLAY BY THE RULES.
YOU DON'T MOVE THE BALL. YOU DON'T PLAY
WINTER RULES. I PLAY GOLF WITH PEOPLE AND
DON'T MOVE THE BALL. THEY ASK ME WHY, I
SAY, "I MIGHT PLAY WITH SPURRIER AGAIN."[16]

—*Lonnie Lowe*

I'D ALMOST RATHER HAVE FOOTBALL BROUGHT
HOME THAN THE GOLF. BECAUSE HE GOES
THROUGH EVERY SHOT. HE CALLS ME ON THE
PHONE ON THE WAY HOME FROM THE GOLF
COURSE AND TELLS ME EVERY SHOT. "AND
THEN ON THE TWELFTH HOLE. . . ."[17]

—*Jerri Spurrier*

REV. GRAHAM SPURRIER, HIS FATHER

He was the first coach I ever had, though he never coached me in football. He was the ultimate competitor. Every game was about playing your best. He hated losing. He probably liked baseball the best of all the sports. He tried not to allow me to get overconfident, the big head.

⌒

My dad taught me a long time ago, "If you keep score, you're supposed to try to win."[18]

⌒

HE WAS STEVE'S COACH, AND WHATEVER STEVE DID WAS NEVER
GOOD ENOUGH. HE PUSHED AND PUSHED AND PUSHED. THAT
DOESN'T WORK WITH EVERYBODY, BUT STEVE COULD HANDLE IT.[19]

—Jerri Spurrier

IMAGE

We're not going to have players that are an embarrassment
to us, it's as simple as that. It's not written down exactly
how you handle everyone because each case is different,
but we're going to have first-class citizens in our program.[20]

JERRI SPURRIER

I think every successful man must have a good wife and
have things in order at home and that certainly has been
the case for me. My family has been healthy and God has
blessed us, for which I am very thankful. Most of it goes
back to Jerri, who is probably the closest thing to being a
perfect coach's wife that exists.[21]

JERRI WAS PRETTY POPULAR HERSELF (AT FLORIDA). SHE DIDN'T
TREAT STEVE LIKE HE WAS THIS ALL-AMERICAN CAMPUS HERO
AND CHASE HIM. I THINK HE HAD TO CHASE JERRI.[22]

—**Fred Goldsmith**, *the witness at
Spurrier's wedding ceremony after the couple eloped*

IT SHOCKED US, BUT IT WORKED OUT. THEY'VE BEEN MARRIED
THIRTY YEARS.[23]

—**Marjorie Spurrier**, *Steve's mother, upon
learning that her son eloped and got married*

LEGACY

I just want to be known as a guy whose pleasure is in
winning championships and doing things the right,
honest way.[24]

I DON'T BELIEVE
COACH SPURRIER
SPENDS A LOT OF TIME
THINKING ABOUT
WHAT HE'S DONE.
HE'S MORE WORRIED
ABOUT WHAT HE'S
ABOUT TO DO.[25]

—*Danny Wuerffel*

LOSING

I get a kick out of people who talk like I've been a winner my whole life. That's just not the way it is. The fact is I was the starting quarterback for the worst team (winless 1976 Tampa Bay Buccaneers) in NFL history. You can't deny it. It happened.[26]

I'm embarrassed about this. After playing Nebraska, I feel if we played them ten times, they'd probably beat us ten times. It was a difficult night and they were just better than us, a lot.

—*after a 62-24 loss to Nebraska in the 1996 Fiesta Bowl*

They're out there laughing. We're in here crying. That's how sports is.

—*following a 40-39 loss to Alabama in 1999 that ended a thirty-game home winning streak*

OFFICIATING

If I say too much about the officiating, it'd make me look like a crybaby, and I certainly don't want to be a crybaby about the officials. But all you've got to do is look at the statistics of how many (penalties) we get compared to the other teams. Something's wrong there.[27]

I probably deserved it.
> —*responding to letter of reprimand from Southeastern Conference for criticizing officials after 38-35 loss to Auburn in 1993*

I've got to cool it. I've got to quit talking about the officiating publicly and go through the proper channels.[28]
> —*after getting reprimanded by the SEC for criticizing officials*

PERSEVERANCE

We were taught in my family that you don't quit things and if I had stopped going out for football, people would say I quit.[29]

~

Basketball teams win by twenty-five to thirty points, baseball teams win games by eleven or twelve runs, and nobody gives it a second thought. Why should football be any different? Nobody will ever accuse us of going into a prevent offense when we get ahead. You can count on that.[30]

~

We will not call a timeout to stop the clock or throw one into the end zone during the last fifteen to twenty seconds of the game, but in the normal course of action, I believe in letting your players play the game. If they score a touchdown, that's what they would like to do. It's the other team's responsibility to stop them. I've been on the opposite side of it; and if the other team wants to score when they are way ahead of me, that's fine. Their players are having fun. That's football.[31]

~

IT'S OUR JOB TO STOP (SPURRIER). IF I CAN GET SIXTY-TWO ON HIM SOME DAY, I WILL.[32]

—**Phil Fulmer**, *Tennessee coach, after a 62-27 loss at Florida*

POSITIVE THINKING

I firmly believe that if you think something is a problem, then it is a problem. One of the biggest problems we've had in the past (at Florida) is we have made excuses and dwelled on what is negative. I was part of that history as a player, and now I hope I'm part of changing it as a coach. Perhaps one day that will be my legacy as the head coach of the Gators.[33]

I'm a big believer in using quotations from successful people. It's something I started back in 1983 with the Tampa Bay Bandits. It helped me and our players then, and it still does today. "Preparation, Persistence, and Positive" are among the primary thoughts in my theory on what it takes to be successful.[34]

When I got the job here (at Florida), people said: "You can't play Auburn and Georgia back-to-back. You can't do this, you can't do that." What we've tried to do is eliminate those excuses. We should be able to do anything we want as long as we work hard enough to accomplish it.[35]

RUNNING UP THE SCORE

There's a bunch of these run-up-the-score experts that say, "Hey, he runs up the score, he doesn't, he does, he doesn't." Now I wish one of those experts would come up with the exact formula, how many points you have to be ahead, with how much time left, before the coach is supposed to say, "No more scoring," and run up the middle and take a knee and quit playing the game. But no one's ever come up with that formula, and I can't figure it out.[36]

SUN TZU, CHINESE WARRIOR/PHILOSOPHER

He talks about how to prepare for battle. How to get his soldiers, his troops, ready to fight their best. When you think about it, head coaches, in a way, are generals of armies. They have to get their players ready, not to go to war, but for battles each Saturday there is a game. And Sun Tzu believed there is a right way to prepare and a wrong way to prepare.[37]

TURNING A TEAM AROUND

The situation (at Florida) was a lot easier because the team hadn't had much success. The players were looking for something new.[38]

WORKLOAD

No, we don't stay in the office until after midnight, but some people can do in fifteen minutes what others will spread over two hours. As a player, I saw so much time wasted. When a coach says he works sixteen hours a day, it's his security blanket. Then when he loses, nobody can say he was outworked.[39]

Me? I don't try to outwork anybody. I'm not that insecure. I don't need the crutch. We work until the job gets done, then we go home to be with our families.[40]

I see coaches more and more not bragging about how hard they work. Charley Pell came in here and told all the Gators, "Our coaches will have rust on their golf clubs and cobwebs on their fishing poles. Nobody is going to outwork our coaches." Most fans would say, "Oh, boy, our coaches are going to work hard." But nowadays, all fans care about is how the team plays on Saturdays. How hard we work doesn't matter, it's how productive we are.[41]

I may work harder than a lot of people think. I know there's that perception that since I play golf and work out six days a week on the treadmill for twenty-five to thirty minutes, that I don't work hard. All coaches have to prepare the way they're comfortable. If you've got a good game plan and your players are ready, you can sit there and watch tape for four or five more hours or you can go home and be with your family. I think that's a good perception to have.

"I may work harder than a lot of people think." Indeed, Spurrier deserves credit for living a balanced life that allows time for family and golf. *(Photo courtesy of University of Florida sports information office)*

If the most hours spent at the office by coaches was the key to winning, a lot of other programs would be winning. To me what's important is making the best use of the time you have with your players, not the time when the coaches are by themselves coming up with schemes and watching film on the other guy. It's what you can teach your players to do that counts. That's the most important part of coaching.[42]

I probably don't come in as early as a lot of coaches and maybe don't stay as late as a lot of coaches, but I'll bet almost anything that I spent more time with our players at Florida last year—I'm talking about the quarterbacks and receivers. I would say as a head coach I was with the players more than probably any other head coach in the country. I'm a big believer that the time you spend with your players who are playing the game is the most important part of coaching.[43]

More Quotes from Others

IF YOU'RE ONE OF THE SKEPTICS WHO HAS BEEN TAKING SHOTS AT STEVE SPURRIER SINCE HE WAS NAMED COACH OF THE REDSKINS, BE AWARE THAT THIS GUY HAS A LONG MEMORY. HECK, HE STILL BRINGS UP WHAT FOLKS SAID ABOUT HIM WHEN HE CAME TO FLORIDA FROM DUKE. ALL HE DID AFTER THAT IS BUILD THE MOST FEARED OFFENSIVE SYSTEM IN COLLEGE FOOTBALL. AND AS FAR AS REVELING IN HIS GOOD OL' BOY TWANG, YOU WOULD DO WELL TO BE CAREFUL WITH THAT. THIS GUY IS AS DUMB AS YOUR AVERAGE FOX.[1]

—**Randy Cross**, *former NFL player*

HE DEFINITELY CHANGED THE SEC AND THE WAY A LOT OF PEOPLE THINK. I'M NOT A GREAT HISTORIAN OF THE LEAGUE, BUT IT ALWAYS SEEMED THAT IF YOU DON'T LEAD THE LEAGUE IN RUSHING, YOU CAN'T WIN THE CONFERENCE. WHEN SOMEBODY COMES IN AND DOES SOMETHING DIFFERENT AND WINS, THEN EVERYBODY FEELS THAT CONVENTIONAL WISDOM MAY NOT BE THE WAY TO GO ANYMORE.[2]

—**Mark Richt**, *Georgia coach*

ONE THING I'M CURIOUS ABOUT: YOU'VE SEEN IT BEFORE, WHERE THOSE QUARTERBACKS ARE LOOKING TO THE SIDELINE AT HIM. I DON'T KNOW HOW THAT'S GOING TO WORK HERE. IT'S THE TIME (BETWEEN PLAYS), AND DEFENSES ARE SO MUCH SMARTER.[3]

—**Peyton Manning**, *Indianapolis Colts quarterback and former QB at Florida rival Tennessee*

THERE PROBABLY WOULD BE A LOT OF PRESSURE IF WE WERE TALK-ING ABOUT ANYBODY BUT STEVE (SPURRIER). I'VE NEVER SEEN ANY-BODY HANDLE PRESSURE THE WAY HE DOES. HE TOLD ME THAT PEOPLE KEEP ASKING HIM ABOUT THE PRESSURE, AND HE KEEPS TELLING THEM THERE IS NONE. THE GUY IS A ROCK.[4]

—**John Reaves**, *former Florida assistant coach, talking about Spurrier's first game as the Gator head coach*

I DON'T THINK THERE EVER WAS A PLAY THAT WAS GIVEN TO STEVE
THAT HE ACCEPTED AT FACE VALUE. HE ALWAYS HAD A BETTER WAY
OF DOING IT. I REMEMBER HIM ARGUING WITH (HALL OF FAME
QUARTERBACK) Y. A. TITTLE, WHO WAS OUR OFFENSIVE COORDINA-
TOR, ABOUT THE PLAYS. IT DIDN'T MATTER WHO YOU WERE. HE'D
RISK OFFENDING ANYBODY WHEN IT CAME TO X'S AND O'S.[5]

*—**Ken Willard**, former San Francisco 49ers teammate*

I'LL GIVE STEVE SPURRIER ANYTHING HE WANTS TO COACH THE
CARDINALS. HE'S THE BEST COACH IN COLLEGE FOOTBALL. STEVE
SPURRIER, PLEASE COME HERE. MR. BIDWILL (ARIZONA CARDINALS
OWNER), PLEASE GIVE STEVE SPURRIER ANYTHING HE WANTS TO
COME HERE AND COACH YOUR FOOTBALL TEAM.[6]

*—**Charles Barkley**, former Phoenix Suns forward,*
after seeing Spurrier at a Suns game prior to the Fiesta Bowl

STEVE HAS MADE A LOT OF PLAYERS GREAT WHO HAVEN'T PLAYED
VERY WELL IN THE NFL. NOW THAT HE'S IN THE NFL, WHO'S TO SAY
HE CAN'T MAKE THESE PLAYERS BETTER?[7]

*—**Kim Helton**, Washington Redskins offensive line coach*

I'VE NEVER SEEN ANYTHING LIKE THE HYPE
SPURRIER GOT COMING TO WASHINGTON SINCE
VINCE LOMBARDI (CAME FROM THE GREEN BAY
PACKERS). I THINK HE CAN CHANGE A TEAM
FOR THE BETTER ALMOST MORE THAN ANY
COACH I'VE SEEN.[8]

—**Bowie Kuhn**, *former baseball
commissioner, a lifelong Redskins fan*

I THINK HE'S ONE OF THE MOST MISUNDERSTOOD
GUYS THAT I'VE EVER COME ACROSS. SOMETIMES
HE SAYS THINGS FROM HIS HEART THAT HE
GENUINELY AND TRULY FEELS AND THAT RUBS
PEOPLE THE WRONG WAY. IF YOU REALLY GET
TO KNOW HIM, HE'S A SIMPLE GUY WITH SIMPLE,
CORRECT VALUES. HE'S NOT A PHONY.

—**Billy Donovan**, *Florida basketball coach*

HE'S ONE HONEST SUCKER. IF I EVER HEARD A
STORY ABOUT HIM IN RECRUITING, I'D NEVER
BELIEVE IT. HE'S ALSO VERY CONFIDENT,
COCKY, AND SOMETIMES THAT'S INTERPRETED
AS ARROGANT. BUT THAT'S WHAT MAKES STEVE
SPURRIER, HIS CONFIDENCE.[9]

—**Lou Holtz**, *South Carolina coach*

HE'S A LOT DIFFERENT (AS A DAD). HE'S MORE
LAID-BACK AND NOT AS SERIOUS. HE'S FUN TO
BE WITH. HE'S NOT ANNOYING. HE CAN BE
VERY FUNNY. THAT PRETTY MUCH SUMS IT UP.[10]

—**Scotty Spurrier**, *Steve's youngest son*

I THINK STEVE WAS BORN TO BE A LEADER. HE WAS A LEADER ON EVERY TEAM HE PLAYED ON. KIDS LOOKED UP TO HIM. I NEVER WENT INTO A GAME WITH HIM THAT I DIDN'T THINK WE WOULD WIN BECAUSE OF HIM. WHEN YOU'RE A KID AND YOU'RE OUT ON THE PLAYGROUND, THERE'S ALWAYS THAT ONE PERSON YOU WANT ON YOUR TEAM. WELL, STEVE WAS THAT PERSON.[11]

—Elvin Little, *Spurrier's high school basketball coach at Science Hill in Johnson City, Tennessee*

STEVE SPURRIER IS A GOD.[12]

—Dave Brown, *former Duke quarterback*

THERE ARE TWO TYPES OF COACHES—THOSE WHO PLAY TO WIN AND THOSE WHO ARE AFRAID TO LOSE. STEVE PLAYS TO WIN. STEVE IS TOTALLY WITHOUT FEAR AND DOESN'T WORRY ABOUT FAILURE. HE'S DANGEROUS BECAUSE HE'LL TAKE A CHANCE.[13]

—Pepper Rodgers, *Washington Redskins administrator and former USFL coaching rival*

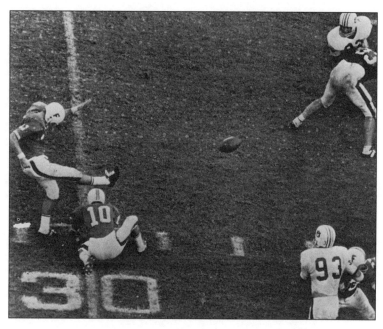

Spurrier boots the winning field goal against Auburn in 1966 that pretty much wrapped up the Heisman Trophy for him. (Photo courtesy of University of Florida sports information office)

JUST LIKE YOU CAN'T JUDGE A BOOK BY
THE DUST JACKET, YOU CAN'T JUDGE
FOOTBALL COACHES BY THEIR EXTERIOR.
I DOUBTED THAT THE UNIVERSITY OF
FLORIDA'S STEVE SPURRIER WOULD EVER BE
A GOOD FOOTBALL COACH BECAUSE HE
LOOKED TOO MUCH LIKE A MALE MODEL
AND EVERYTHING CAME EASY TO HIM.
OUTSTANDING ATHLETES SOMETIMES AREN'T
GOOD COACHES BECAUSE THEY USUALLY
AREN'T ABLE TO RELATE TO THE LESS
BLESSED. SPURRIER HAS FOOLED US ALL.[14]

—*Furman Bisher*, Atlanta Journal *columnist*

A whole lot of Spurriers goin' 'round, circa 2000. Front row, left to right: grandsons Jake Moody, Davis King, and Trey King, and son Scotty Spurrier. Seated: daughter Ann Moody holding Kyle Moody, Jerri Spurrier holding grandson Gavin Spurrier, Steve holding granddaughter Emma Spurrier, and daughter-in-law Melissa Spurrier holding Luke Spurrier. Standing: son-in-law Jay Moody, daughter Lisa King, son-in-law Emerson King, and Steve Spurrier Jr. (Photo courtesy of University of Florida sports information office)

Notes

Playing Days

1. *Lakeland Ledger*, November 20, 1996.
2. Ibid., November 13, 1996.
3. Ibid., November 14, 1996.
4. *Florida Times-Union*, December 10, 1993.
5. *Lakeland Ledger*, November 14, 1996.
6. *Tampa Tribune*, December 8, 1995.
7. Ibid., August 27, 1995.
8. Ibid.
9. *Florida Times-Union*, December 10, 1967.
10. *Jacksonville Journal*, May 4, 1984.
11. *Lakeland Ledger*, November 15, 1996.
12. Ibid.
13. *San Francisco Chronicle*, January 14, 1994.
14. *Jacksonville Journal*, May 6, 1976.
15. Associated Press, March 8, 1977.
16. *Florida Times-Union*, April 14, 1977.
17. United Press International, June 2, 1977.
18. Associated Press, August 30, 1977.
19. *Lakeland Ledger*, November 15, 1996.
20. Ibid., November 16, 1996.

Career Moves

1. *Denver Post*, December 31, 1995.
2. *Saint Petersburg Times*, November 19, 1989.
3. *Gainesville Sun*, August 26, 2001.
4. *Jacksonville Journal*, December 20, 1977.
5. Associated Press, October 8, 1984.
6. *Florida Times-Union*, November 26, 1989.

7. *The National*, October 25, 1990.

8. *Gainesville Sun*, August 26, 2001.

9. Associated Press, January 9, 1987.

10. Spurrier, Steve, with Norm Carlson, *Gators: The Inside Story of Florida's First SEC Title*. Orlando, FL: Tribune Publishing, 1992.

11. *Fort Lauderdale-Sun Sentinel*, January 19, 1993.

12. *Orlando Sentinel*, December 16, 1993.

13. Ibid., January 5, 2002.

14. *Jacksonville Journal*, December 22, 1981.

15. *Florida Times Union*, November 22, 1986.

16. Ibid., October 9, 1984.

17. Ibid., November 26, 1989.

18. *Tampa Tribune*, January 10, 1996.

19. *Florida Times-Union*, January 10, 1996.

20. *Palm Beach Post*, June 29, 1994.

21. *Lakeland Ledger*, November 16, 1996.

22. *Jacksonville Journal*, December 7, 1978.

23. *Sports Illustrated*, October 23, 1995.

24. *Lakeland Ledger*, November 16, 1996.

25. Ibid.

26. Ibid., November 17, 1996.

27. Spurrier and Carlson.

28. *Lakeland Ledger*, November 17, 1996.

29. *Florida Times-Union*, July 4, 1983.

30. *Lakeland Ledger*, November 17, 1996.

31. Ibid.

32. United Press International, June 17, 1985.

33. *Tampa Tribune*, October 11, 1995.

34. *Bergen Record*, March 24, 1985.

35. Associated Press, August 5, 1986.

36. *Lakeland Ledger*, November 17, 1996.

37. *Saint Petersburg Times*, August 31, 1994.

38. *Charleston Sunday Gazette Mail*, January 2, 1994.

39. *Gainesville Sun*, August 29, 1999.
40. *Palm Beach Post*, April 20, 1995.

Blue Devils to Gators
1. *Florida Times-Union*, November 26, 1989.
2. *Saint Petersburg Times*, March 3, 1987.
3. *Florida Times-Union*, December 2, 1995.
4. *Lakeland Ledger*, November 20, 1996.
5. Ibid., November 18, 1996.
6. Spurrier, Steve, with Norm Carlson, *Gators: The Inside Story of Florida's First SEC Title*. Orlando, FL: Tribune Publishing, 1992.
7. *Saint Petersburg Times*, September 6, 1987.
8. *Washington Post*, January 20, 2002.
9. *Saint Petersburg Times*, November 19, 1989.
10. Ibid.
11. *Florida Times-Union*, November 19, 1989.
12. *Lakeland Ledger*, November 18, 1996.
13. *Florida Times-Union*, November 13, 1978.
14. Ibid., January 1, 1990.
15. *The National*, October 25, 1990.
16. *Orange County Register*, December 29, 1989.
17. *Saint Petersburg Times*, November 29, 1989.
18. Ibid., November 11, 1994.
19. *Gainesville Sun*, June 9, 1992.
20. *Saint Petersburg Times*, November 18, 1993.
21. Ibid..
22. *Gainesville Sun*, September 9, 1997.
23. *Florida Times-Union*, November 26, 1989.
24. *Gainesville Sun*, October 3, 1998.
25. CBS Sportsline.com, March 3, 2002.
26. *New York Times*, November 26, 1996.
27. *Gainesville Sun*, January 10, 2002.
28. Ibid.

Opponents, Rivalries, and Smirks

1. Spurrier, Steve, with Norm Carlson, *Gators: The Inside Story of Florida's First SEC Title*. Orlando, FL: Tribune Publishing, 1992.
2. *Florida Times-Union*, July 25, 1993.
3. Ibid., October 31, 1992.
4. Ibid.
5. Ibid.
6. *Atlanta Constitution*, November 4, 1992.
7. *Palm Beach Post*, October 29, 1995.
8. *Florida Times-Union*, November 21, 1994.
9. Ibid., February 5, 1993.
10. *Florida Today*, January 7, 2002.
11. *Virginian-Pilot*, February 3, 1995.
12. *Bob Griese's College Football 1997*.
13. Knight-Ridder Newspapers, January 1, 1990.
14. *Washington Post*, January 16, 2002.
15. *Orlando Sentinel*, March 24, 2002.
16. *Atlanta Journal and Constitution*, August 11, 1992.
17. *Sports Illustrated* special edition, January 1997.

Quarterbacks and Pitching It Around

1. *Fort Lauderdale Sun-Sentinel*, August 31, 1995.
2. SportingNews.com, May 2, 2002.
3. Ibid.
4. *Florida Times-Union*, September 14, 1991.
5. Spurrier, Steve, with Norm Carlson, *Gators: The Inside Story of Florida's First SEC Title*. Orlando, FL: Tribune Publishing, 1992.
6. *Saint Petersburg Times,* December 28, 1993.
7. 1992 Florida media guide.
8. *Sports Illustrated*, October 23, 1995.
9. *Miami Herald*, August 29, 1996.
10. *Florida Times-Union*, September 14, 1991.
11. Spurrier and Carlson.
12. Ibid.

13. *Jacksonville Journal*, November 14, 1978.
14. *Florida Times-Union*, October 8, 1995.
15. *Philadelphia Daily News*, October 13, 1995.
16. *Lakeland Ledger*, November 21, 1996.
17. *Florida Times-Union*, September 14, 1991.
18. Ibid.
19. *New Orleans Times-Picayune*, December 4, 1994.
20. *Washington Post*, January 15, 2002.
21. *USA Today*, November 27, 1990.
22. *Lindy's Sports Annuals, 12 Years of Dominance*, D.M.D. Publications, Inc., Birmingham, AL, January 2002.
23. *Washington Post*, December 3, 1989.
24. *Chicago Tribune*, December 31, 1995.
25. *Florida Times-Union*, November 26, 1989.
26. Spurrier and Carlson.
27. *Sports Illustrated*, October 23, 1995.
28. *Jacksonville Journal*, June 11, 1980.
29. *Bob Griese's College Football 1997*.
30. Spurrier and Carlson.
31. *Atlanta Constitution*, December 2, 1994.

The NFL and the Redskins

1. *Washington Post*, January 15, 2002.
2. *Gainesville Sun*, January 5, 2002.
3. *Washington Post*, January 27, 2002.
4. Associated Press, May 16, 2002.
5. *Sports Illustrated*, March 25, 2002.
6. *Orlando Sentinel*, March 24, 2002.
7. *Lindy's Sports Annuals, 12 Years of Dominance*, D.M.D. Publications, Inc., Birmingham, AL, January 2002.
8. *Sports Illustrated*, March 25, 2002.
9. *Washington Post*, January 20, 2002.
10. *Sports Illustrated*, March 25, 2002.

11. *Orlando Sentinel*, January 16, 2002.

12. *Washington Post*, January 15, 2002.

13. Ibid., January 20, 2002.

14. *New York Times*, March 31, 2002.

15. ESPN interview, April 21, 2002.

16. Ibid.

17. *Washington Post*, April 21, 2002.

18. Associated Press, January 15, 2002.

19. *Washington Post*, February 7, 2002.

20. Ibid., October 16, 1993.

21. Ibid., January 16, 2002.

22. *Houston Chronicle*, August 28, 1994.

Spurrier His Own Self

1. Spurrier, Steve, with Norm Carlson, *Gators: The Inside Story of Florida's First SEC Title*. Orlando, FL: Tribune Publishing, 1992.

2. *Fort Lauderdale Sun-Sentinel*, December 31, 1995.

3. Ibid.

4. *Orlando Sentinel*, February 6, 1992.

5. *Houston Chronicle*, August 28, 1994.

6. *Orlando Sentinel*, June 19, 1997.

7. *Saint Petersburg Times*, November 12, 1994.

8. *Sports Illustrated*, October 23, 1995.

9. *Palm Beach Post*, August 30, 2001.

10. *Sports Illustrated*, October 23, 1995.

11. *Washington Post*, January 20, 2002.

12. Ibid.

13. *Orlando Sentinel*, November 25, 1992.

14. *Palm Beach Post*, December 10, 1995.

15. *College Sports* magazine, November 1994.

16. *Miami Herald*, August 29, 1994.

17. *American Football Monthly*, December 2001.

18. Ibid.

19. *Atlanta Journal and Constitution*, July 19, 1992.
20. *College Sports* magazine, November 1994.
21. Ibid.
22. *Sports Illustrated*, October 23, 1995.
23. Spurrier and Carlson.
24. United Press International, May 9, 1978.
25. Spurrier and Carlson.
26. CBS Sportsline.com, March 3, 2002.
27. *Orlando Sentinel*, November 24, 1995.
28. *Saint Petersburg Times*, November 11, 1994.
29. *Lakeland Ledger*, November 22, 1996.
30. Ibid.
31. *Atlanta Constitution*, December 2, 1994.
32. Ibid.
33. *Palm Beach Post*, August 10, 1997.
34. *Atlanta Journal and Constitution*, October 28, 1992.
35. *Chicago Tribune*, December 5, 1993.

Alphabet Steve
 1. *Lakeland Ledger*, November 22, 1996.
 2. *College Sports* magazine, November 1994.
 3. *Gator Bait*, November 19, 1998.
 4. *College Sports* magazine, November 1994.
 5. *Saint Petersburg Times*, August 26, 1990.
 6. *Florida Times-Union*, January 11, 1996.
 7. Ibid., December 25, 1996.
 8. Ibid.
 9. *Lakeland Ledger*, November 22, 1996.
10. Ibid.
11. Spurrier, Steve, with Norm Carlson, *Gators: The Inside Story of Florida's First SEC Title*. Orlando, FL: Tribune Publishing, 1992.
12. Ibid.
13. *Jacksonville Journal*, March 29, 1979.

14. Spurrier and Carlson.
15. *Orlando Sentinel*, November 26, 1989.
16. *Florida Times Union*, October 14, 1994.
17. *Lakeland Ledger*, November 22, 1996.
18. *Washington Post*, January 20, 2002.
19. *Sports Illustrated*, October 23, 1995.
20. *Florida Times-Union*, August 30, 1992.
21. Spurrier and Carlson.
22. *Lakeland Ledger*, November 14, 1996.
23. Ibid.
24. *Denver Post*, December 31, 1995.
25. *Atlanta Journal-Constitution*, December 31, 1995.
26. *Florida Times-Union*, July 28, 1995.
27. Ibid., November 1, 1993.
28. *Gainesville Sun*, November 2, 1993.
29. *Washington Post*, January 20, 2002.
30. Spurrier and Carlson.
31. Ibid.
32. *New York Daily News*, September 17, 1995.
33. Spurrier and Carlson.
34. Ibid.
35. *Saint Petersburg Times*, November 18, 1993.
36. *Orlando Sentinel*, November 24, 1995.
37. *Athlon Sports, College Football 1999*.
38. *Florida Times-Union*, August 30, 1992.
39. *Saint Petersburg Times*, November 19, 1989.
40. Ibid.
41. *Gainesville Sun*, August 29, 1999.
42. *American Football Monthly*, December 2001.
43. ESPN interview, April 21, 2002.

More Quotes from Others

1. Sporting News.com, March 21, 2002.
2. *Lindy's Sports Annuals, 12 Years of Dominance*, D.M.D. Publications, Inc., Birmingham, Ala., January 2002.
3. *USA Today*, May 22, 2002.
4. *Saint Petersburg Times*, September 8, 1990.
5. *Florida Times-Union*, December 28, 1991.
6. Ibid., December 31, 1995.
7. *Orlando Sentinel*, March 3, 2002.
8. *Florida Times-Union*, April 6, 2002.
9. GoGamecocks.com, November 8, 2001.
10. *Gainesville Sun*, June 18, 2000.
11. *Lakeland Ledger*, November 11, 1996.
12. *Miami Herald*, August 29, 1996.
13. *Charleston Sunday Gazette Mail*, January 2, 1994.
14. *Atlanta Journal*, December 6, 1995.